Speak with an

Irish Brogue

by Ivan Borodin

Illustrations by Pete Sain

ISBN-13: 978-1502572080

ISBN-10: 1502572087

Introduction

I began teaching accents and dialects before the widespread adoption of the internet, so it seems odd to begin a book by justifying its need. With the advent of the smartphone, anyone can tap their screen and find a video lesson on this and nearly any accent.

There's a lot of money being spent nowadays on 'experience' vacations, where the adventurous risk their lives, getting high from elevated adrenaline levels. Is it just me, or is society growing increasingly intense?

This book is meant to be the antidote to crash-course fever. It is intended to provide a relaxed tour of the Irish brogue.

The chapters outline a 'general' Irish sound, so the performer is initiated into speaking with a brogue. If an actor is given an Irish role, this manual makes an excellent starting point to rally from.

The Irish brogue has the vintage feel of the hard-candy shell of Studebakers and Corvettes. The dialect evokes images of courtyards with rose bushes, spraying fountains and circular staircases that lead to views which prove the climb worthwhile.

Enjoy the explanations and examples in this book. Settle in and let the magic of the Irish brogue affect your speech. You'll cross the rainbow bridge in no time, a lilt rising in your voice, glittering like the metaphoric pot of gold. I hope you'll consider this handbook your lucky charm.

Placement of the Irish Sound

Irish speech tends to sound tighter then that of American English. There is a slight nasality attachedto the accent, as well as a rising in pitch. While the American accent tends to resonate off of the jaw (US- 'I'll *call* you in a *few days'*), the Irish sound tends to spring from behind the upper teeth, behind the area above the upper lip, where one might grow a mustache (IRISH - 'I *shall* call you in a few *days'*).

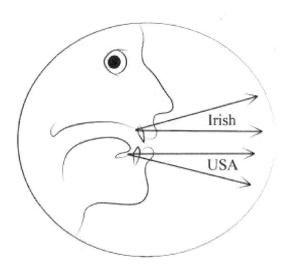

3

The Long I starts with an intrusive 'uh' sound

This key vowel demonstrates how the Irish resonance grows from behind the upper teeth. This is very different from American English. The vowel is generated higher in the face, tightening it, darkening its stem. The Irishman rises in pitch on stressed sounds, so this long vowel will ascend in pitch when emphasized.

high, die, while, like

The *knights* were *driving* straight into the storm.

We're wondering *why* they never *tried* to do what we're doing.

Enough talk, 'tis *time* to take action.

Witness the *final* performance.

4

Those billboards *might* be overly dramatic, but so far they're *right.*

The entertainment factor will not dim in the *slightest.*

Some cultures believe in the trickery of *spiders.*

The *sky* was dark and *Michael* could see the *line* where the snow had started to fall.

Brian commissioned the most interesting *variety* of *writers* he could *find.*

'Twas *five*-forty-*five* and still dark *outside.*

Put the *light* on when you read your *Bible.*

There was a long *silence* on the other end of the *line.*

We will not ask anyone to forgive our *crimes*.

6

7

The Long U rises in pitch

The American speaker descends in pitch on stressed syllables. Irish speakers do the opposite, rising in pitch on points of emphasis. This upward lilt is particularly noticeable on the Long U.

presumably, refused, therapeutic, consumer, tool, doing, unions

Who were *you two* with?

Judith assumed what they told her was *true*.

I *knew* a lot of good people with that *tattoo*.

Bruce ushered them into a *pew* at the rear of the chapel.

Derived from the Latin word for *glue, gluten* is *used* in hair spray, lipstick and moisturizers.

'Tis not the *truth* of *who* we are.

8

She *used* the *wound* as an *excuse* to *improve* her *beauty.*

I *grew* to see bad *news* as *opportunities* for growth.

9

The Long A rises in pitch

According to Irish folklore, a pot of gold waits at the end of each rainbow. To claim that treasure, you need to follow the rainbow's path. To sound Irish, you will need to go upward in pitch on stressed syllables.

great, maybe, case, day, bay, brain, baked

That style of *play* seems genius when you *occasionally* win.

Then *came* the *unmistakable* warning that accompanies all equipment *engaged* in reverse.

In my feeling of *nakedness*, I *prayed* desperately for something to *take place.*

The *way* she was *saving* money *made* him *change* his attitude towards her.

Instead of sitting *straight* in his seat, he *feigned* fatigue and leaned against the *table.*

10

She *mainly* hung out with people from distant *places*.

He felt *impatient* about the big *date* at the *café*.

Amy hated to *waste* a *paper* towel on cleaning *plates*.

Let's *make* our *escape* to that *neighboring* apartment.

11

The Long O rises in pitch

Like the other long vowels, the long O ascends in pitch when emphasized by an Irish speaker. Keep the O pure, avoiding an intrusive 'eah' at its start, which would create a British air.

For example (this is an example of British speech):

    eah-O   *eah-O*
Did you know it's bad luck to toast with water?

Defend from sounding British by maintaining a pure long O (the arrow is a reminder to ascend in pitch).

      ↗   ↗
Did you know 'tis bad luck to toast with water?

woke, commotion, don't, old, most

She confided to him in a *low* whisper.

They took the *cold* as permission to edge *closer* to each other.

Use *bold* colors to *show* a pattern of defiance.

What would it be like to come *home* to that?

They hauled *overnight* bags and *groceries* into the new house.

He *negotiated* with the plumber about replacing the *corroded* pipe.

She rested her chin on his *shoulder*.

Catching a *solar* eclipse from a *sofa* is a sad *joke*.

The sensations crashed *over* me at unexpected *moments*.

The Short U leans toward OO

There is a slight nasality to the Irish Brogue. While the American accent resonates off the jaw, the Irish sound springs from behind the upper teeth, the area above the upper lip where a lad might grow a moustache.

swung, become, perfunctory, understand, once

He *wondered sometimes* what she needed from him.

Could *one* list the reasons why they *loved someone*?

Time is *money* to *truck* drivers.

The phone *rung* before the crack of dawn and woke me *up*.

'Potato *bug' is another* name for that type of grasshopper.

The correct answer *won somebody* a new *oven.*

The only *customers* in the *pub* were *some* kids shooting pool.

Hunter wandered the *countryside* for the past several *months.*

Justin sees death *rushing* toward him.

Douglas threw too many *punches* during the brawl.

A blazing figure *cuts* through the icy void of space.

16

17

The Short A leans toward the Short O

The Irish brogue is often described as 'breathy', meaning that it seems lighter than American English. This vowel change is partly responsible for creating that impression.

Do not attempt to force extra air through the vocal cords. This vowel substitution should cover the so-called 'breathiness'.

mechanical, thanks, language, actually, grab, attack

Abigail is making a big deal out of the *fact* that *Jack* didn't feel like dancing.

I'll get my *magazine back* from *Patrick* and see whose career is more pathetic.

18

Couldn't *Janet* talk *Zachary* into leaving the *blackjack* table?

Dad says *that*'s the starting *salary.*

Brad must really believe in my *talent.*

They called *last* week for your social security number.

It turned out Morrisey *had* eleven items *after* all.

You seem like you're *having* a *fantastic* evening.

20

OU leans toward AU

In American English, words spelled OU (as in 'out') and OW (as in 'down') are frequently based on the short A (as in 'cat'). Irish speakers begin this sound with a short O (as in 'not').

Despite the way this sound is annotated in dictionaries, Americans pronounce it:
(USA) down, around, shower.

The Irishman starts this sound with a short O:
(IRI) down, around, shower

(American) down   (Irish) down
(American) around   (Irish) around
(American) shower   (Irish) shower

The moment you hear this change, you can detect that the speaker is Irish.

22

wow, about

The *coward* left *town* and stopped her alimony payments.

Ireland is a land filled with delights unlike any others *found* in the world.

I recognize it *now*.

He's *bound* to spot me long before I reach the mansion.

Fog had settled over the *house* like a *shroud*.

The road *wound* parallel with the river.

He's coming *out* of the *tower.*

24

25

The Long E rises in pitch

Continuing on our ambitious path to add the Irish brogue to your list of accents, I present to you the most common of English vowels, the long E. Use this prevalent vowel to convince your listener. Rise in pitch when the long E is emphasized.

between, being, knees, these, female, teeth, street, field, steel, senior, trees, phoenix

Keep the focus on what you truly *need*.

A *three*-day celebration drew *thirteen* million *people* and *even featured* an elaborate *speech*.

Let's take a behind-the-*scenes* look at some of the *key* elements of this landmark.

The tile is primarily *geometric* and the *ceiling motifs* are more abstract floral.

My *feelings* for *Eve* left me confused about my intentions.

I haven't *seen* or corresponded with him in *weeks*.

The one person I know is daft is *me*.

He is a *key* figure in the *automobile* industry.

The story of how this came to *be* is my darkest *secret.*

I *guarantee* that *Steve* won't *believe* it *either.*

The will stipulates that the following *people be* present.

It *seemed* that the *sweet* woman *received* an *immediate* response.

I *feel* like *we need* an *increased* level of awareness.

The vein in his temples swelled like a *piece* of blue cord.

When the long E appears in the 'EA' combination, the Irish speaker tends to interpret it as a long A.

leaned, meat, eat, meal, weaker, tea, beach, scream, teach, east, peaceful

He's yet to *beat* a *team* that finished the *season* in the top ten.

I never would have *dreamed* of getting mad at him before.

One of the station's most unifying *features* is its tile work.

Let me *leave* the decision to you.

What's the *real reason* for *cleaning* your kitchen?

He was quite irritated with the *speaker*.

Let's *read* this and *deal* with the facts as they are.

What does that *mean* for us?

Having found *each* other at last, they come before us
to join in the most sacred and honored union.

30

EAH becomes the Short A

In American English, when the short A appears before the letters M and N, the sound is likely to be influenced by those consonants.

(USA) I just *can't* believe it. Be the *man.*

That sound change is a telltale sign of an American accent. When spoken by an Irishman, the sound remains a short A.

(Ireland) I just *can't* believe it. Be the *man.*

ante, stand, hand, transfer, chance, glanced

That *brand* of *shampoo* promises to *enhance* natural tones.

Randall answered all of *Dan's* questions.

32

How are you *handling* the growing list of *demands*?

My *grandparents* claim to suffer *cramps*.

Do you *understand* the *example?*

I *am* where I *am* on this path, and *can't* be anywhere else.

Plans were *expanded* to renovate the *abandoned* building.

Reflections *danced* and shimmered on the surface of the water.

These *dandelions* really *stand* out from the rest.

34

35

'R' endings

Irish 'R' endings resemble those in American English. In both cases, the tip of the tongue moves back as an 'R' ending is uttered, but when an Irishman stresses an 'R' ending, the syllable tends to rise in pitch.

where, smart, firm, chair

Gary slid the *car* into *first gear* and glided out of the *parking* lot.

There were some *workers* in the *yard* at the *warehouse*.

There was an entrance *near* the front of *Caroline's* office.

The *article* about the *fire* must be in by five, *Arthur*.

Street gang violence has grown *serious* in this *area*.

The *deer turned* and *stared* at the sound of the *tires*.

OR becomes AR

Many words that are written OR are sometimes pronounced by the Irishman as AR.

Keep in mind that the greatest distinction between American R-endings and Irish R-endings is that the Irish rise in pitch on stressed syllables.

forties, corpse, explore, board, orange, core

Nancy talked about her passion for a little-respected *form* of fiction.

This makes them an *important source*.

The convention *organizers* paid the expenses.

These people have a higher profile and are *more* well known.

The *northern* sky was *forked* with lightning.

Her makeup collected at the *corners* of her mouth.

I was *born before* an audience of nursing students.

He shared some of his most painful *stories.*

They lost their fancy jobs and were *forced* to relocate.

He was revealed to be hot-tempered and self-*absorbed.*

The Ancient Gaelic festival of Samhain marked the end of summer and start of the New Year, when livestock was chosen for slaughter. Spirit fairies known as the Aos Si could best enter the living world during those two nights, and offerings of food were left. Souls of the deceased returned home, and feasts were held. Spiritually protective bonfires were celebrated. People visited door to door, wearing guises and reciting verses for treats.

The date, October 31.

Mastery Lesson #1
Larry Warns the Inspector

This speech is taken from "Pandora 2012: Southern Belles."

The basic premise of the novel is that a shopping center exists where fantasies come to life. This extremely dangerous place is known as Pandora's Box (sometimes referred to as 'Pandora' or 'The Box').

Larry is a veteran guide at Pandora. When an attractive inspector investigates Larry's operation, he takes her outside his office to issue a warning.

Read the following speech once, attempting your best Irish accent.

40

Larry Warns the Inspector

I wasn't born in the Carolinas. I'm an Irishman. Every once in a blue moon, a tourist asks if I miss my homeland. A day like today, I stretch out my arms and tell them they can keep Ireland. Heck, let them paint a crescent moon on the roof of my Oldsmobile, and tune the horn to sing "Dixie".

You're not the first official to visit the Box. I must have locked horns with a dozen. They generally come in three shapes: pencil sharpeners, badge flashers, and gunslingers. Doesn't matter which flavor of bubble gum they chew, it always ends badly—in ways they don't see coming.

I want you to take this in the right spirit. Trying to regulate the Box is like trying to win a spelling bee by dipping a spoon into alphabet soup. And the reason I brought you outside was to emphasize my point.

Sweetheart, 'tis too beautiful a morning to buy the farm.

41

Consider how the Long I is produced by the Irish speaker, who changes it to uh-I (The Long I will be annotated in the texts as *uh-I).*

uh-I

I wasn't born in the *Carolinas.*

   uh-I
I'm an *Irishman.*

I stretch out my arms and tell them they can keep

uh-I
Ireland.

   uh-I   *uh-I*
Trying to regulate the Box is like *trying* to win a spelling bee by dipping a spoon into alphabet soup.

                                      uh-I
Sweetheart, 'tis too beautiful a morning to *buy* the farm.

42

The Short U becomes OO as in *look* (and will be marked *oo* in the texts).

      oo
Every *once* in a blue moon, a tourist asks if I miss my homeland.

   oo   *oo*
I *must* have locked horns with a *dozen*.

             oo
They generally *come* in three shapes: pencil

               oo
sharpeners, badge flashers, and *gunslingers*.

 oo   *oo*   *oo*
Doesn't matter which flavor of *bubble gum* they chew, it always ends badly—in ways they don't see

 oo
coming.

43

The Short A becomes the Short O (which will be marked in the text as *ah)*.

                                 ah
Every once in a blue moon, a tourist *asks* if I miss my homeland.

They   generally   come   in   three   shapes: pencil

                  ah   *ah*
sharpeners, *badge flashers*, and gunslingers.

              ah
Doesn't *matter* which flavor of bubble gum they

                        ah
chew, it always ends *badly*.

Trying to regulate the Box is like trying to win a

                            ah
spelling bee by dipping a spoon into *alphabet* soup.

In this final reading of the text, aim for the featured changes.

44

Mastery Lesson #1
(with annotations)

uh-I   *uh-I*
I wasn't born in the Carolinas. I'm an Irishman. Every

oo   *ah*
once in a blue moon, a tourist asks if I miss my

homeland. A day like today, I stretch out my arms and

                   uh-I
tell them they can keep Ireland. Heck, let them paint a

crescent moon on the roof of my Oldsmobile, and

tune the horn to sing "Dixie".

                                  oo
You're not the first official to visit the Box. I must

                oo   *oo*
have locked horns with a dozen. They generally come

                         ah   *ah*
in three shapes: pencil sharpeners, badge flashers,

     oo   *oo*   *ah*
and gunslingers. Doesn't matter which flavor of

oo   *ah*
bubble gum they chew, it always ends badly—in

45

oo
ways they don't see coming.

uh-I   *uh-I*
I want you to take this in the right spirit. Trying to

uh-I
regulate the Box is like trying to win a spelling bee by

ah
dipping a spoon into alphabet soup. And the reason I

brought you outside was to emphasize my point.

uh-I
Sweetheart, 'tis too beautiful a morning to buy the

farm.

46

47

Mastery Lesson #2

Sebastian Warns a Tourist

This mastery lesson reviews key vowel and consonant changes, applying them to a monologue, with the goal of helping the speaker nail down the most important aspects of the Irish brogue—the factors crucial to coloring their tones with an emerald radiance.

This monologue is taken from "Pandora 2014: Blood Drive."

Sebastian is a guide at Pandora. In this speech, he tries to convince a woman not to visit the Box.

Read the text, attempting your best Irish accent.

48

Sebastian Warns a Tourist

What my co-workers are trying to relate to you, Abigail, is that whatever logic you've used to justify this excursion won't stack up once we enter Pandora. We had a real genius in here a while back. He figured he could bring President Kennedy back from the dead. Don't laugh. This tourist had done his homework. Exhumed every little-known fact. Exposed every conspiracy theory. He sat right where you are, sipping coffee from this very mug. Articulate guy. He had me believing it could be done. So we strolled into the former Crescent Beach Mall, which on that day strangely resembled a book depository. Outside the Box, my Cadillac became a convertible. We had drinks at Dixie Pride with Lee Harvey Oswald and Jack Ruby. The First Lady gave us a tour of the White House. I even shook hands with Kennedy himself. Well, the tourist and I eventually left Pandora, drove back to the office, and checked online to see if history had been rewritten. Poked around the internet. Know what had changed? Not a damn thing.

49

Use R-endings to generate the accent. Irish emphasis rises in pitch, and this is particularly evident on R-endings.

During this lesson, and on its final runthrough, an arrow aiming diagonally upward (↗) remind the student to ascend in pitch.

↗   ↗   ↗
former, Harvey, word

                                                    ↗
Whatever logic you've used to justify this *excursion*

                              ↗
won't stack up once we enter *Pandora*.

                        ↗
My Cadillac became a *convertible*.

        ↗   ↗
The *First* Lady gave us a *tour* of the White House.

The long O remains a pure vowel. It should not change to eah-O, otherwise the speaker may sound British. In order to prevent the long O from sounding American, it should rise in pitch.

co-worker, won't, drove, so

Don't laugh. This tourist had done his *homework.*

Exhumed every little-*known* fact. *Exposed* every conspiracy theory.

Poked around the internet. *Know* what had changed?

51

The long I takes on an *uh* sound before it, turning it from a pure vowel to *uh-I.*

uh-I   uh-I   uh-I
trying, guy, outside,

                    uh-I
We had a real genius in here a *while* back.

        uh-I
He sat *right* where you are.

                uh-I
We had drinks at Dixie *Pride.*

            uh-I
Well, the tourist and *I* eventually left Pandora, drove

                    uh-I
back to the office, and checked *online.*

Now put it all together, moving patiently through the speech, aiming to use the key vowel changes to affect a convincing Irish brogue.

The operative concept is that mastery over a basic text leads to greater proficiency—both with dialogue and improvised speech.

Mastery Lesson #2 - Sebastian Warns a Tourist
Final Reading

uh-I
What my co-workers are trying to relate to you,

Abigail, is that whatever logic you've used to justify

this excursion won't stack up once we enter Pandora.

We had a real genius in here a while back. He

figured he could bring President Kennedy back from

the dead. Don't laugh. This tourist had done his

homework. Exhumed every little-known fact.

Exposed every conspiracy theory. He sat right where

you are, sipping coffee from this very mug.
uh-I
Articulate guy. He had me believing it could be

done. So we strolled into the former Crescent Beach

Mall, which on that day strangely resembled a book

depository. Outside the Box, my Cadillac became a
↗   *uh-I*
convertible. We had drinks at Dixie Pride with Lee
↗   ↗
Harvey Oswald and Jack Ruby. The First Lady gave
↗   *uh-I*
us a tour of the White House. I even shook hands

↗   *uh-I*
with Kennedy himself. Well, the tourist and I
↗   ↗
eventually left Pandora, drove back to the office, and

uh-I
checked online to see if history had been rewritten.
↗   ↗
Poked around the internet. Know what had changed?

Not a damn thing.

Mastery Lesson #3

This lesson is designed to help the speaker affect a masterful Irish brogue, based on the premise that command over a text translates to fluency with a dialect.

This speech is taken from "Pandora 2011: Accounts of the Cursed Shopping Center."

In this passage, a man knows he is about to lose his girlfriend to her ex, so he explains to that ex how unstable the girl in question has become.

Read the following speech once, attempting your best Irish accent.

56

Mastery Lesson #3

(Mortimer warns Vladi about Alison's fragile nature)

I'm here about Alison. I don't know where to begin. I've had a wee bit to drink.

I know that you and her have this long history. You were a large part of her life for a stretch, and now you're here for her. I'm not daft. Right now she says she hates you, that you should die, and she never wants to see you again. That's what she says right now. But I know that one of these nights she'll be right where I am, looking you over with a nostalgic ache in her heart. I thought I'd beat her to the punch and come see you first.

I knew the whole story. I knew you left her. I always figured you'd come back. But there are parts of this that you aren't aware of.

Alison cracked up when you left. She refused to eat. Had to be locked away for months. I met her last year when her mother passed, and Alison hadn't been with anyone else. In six years, no one since you. Now, I deal with grief every day. People walk into my shop in terrible states. But I see those people bounce back. Even during the brief process of arranging a funeral, people begin to heal. Not so with Alison. The girl is shaky. There are days when I leave the house, and I don't know if she's going to be there when I get back. I've buried many people. I don't want to add her to my list.

I'm older than you. I've seen things I didn't care to. They made me learn to look at a situation for what it is. As much as it hurts, I can admit that Alison isn't in love with me.

If you win Alison back, so be it. I'll let her go. But if you came here for kicks, to seduce her and then pull your vanishing act, I'm warning you I won't take kindly to it. Another disappointment would kill her. If I have to bury her, I'll cremate your skinny ass and dump your ashes.

58

Consider how the short A (as in *had* and *daft*) becomes the short O (as in *not* and *rob*).

This change will be annotated with *ah* as that closely approximates the American short O.

   ah   *ah* *ah* *ah*   *ah*
cracked, back, add, vanishing act

        ah   *ah*
I met her *last* year when her mother *passed*, and

ah   *ah*
Alison hadn't been with anyone else.

    ah   *ah*
If I *have* to bury her, I'll cremate your skinny *ass* and

      ah
dump your *ashes*.

59

Take advantage of R-endings by establishing an upward inflection.

↗ ↗ ↗ ↗ ↗ ↗ ↗
heart, years, girl, care, learn, hurts, warning

↗ ↗ ↗
There are *part*s of this that you *aren't aware* of.

↗ ↗
You were a *large part* of her life for a stretch, and

↗
now you're *here* for her.

60

Words spelled 'OU' are pronounced 'AU' by Irish speakers.

This change will be annotated by *au*, an approximation of the sound.

    au
about

     au
Right *now* she says she hates you.

       au
I see those people *bounce* back.

            au
There are days when I leave the *house*, and I don't know if she's going to be there when I get back.

61

Capitalize on the meaty presence of the long U, which the Irish speaker raises in pitch.

I *knew* the whole story. I *knew* you left her.

She *refused* to eat.

Even during the brief process of arranging a *funeral*, people begin to heal.

If you came here for kicks, to *seduce* her and then pull your vanishing act, I'm warning you I won't take kindly to it.

This is the ultimate lesson of this manual. The goal is to bring everything together. Cast a powerful spell over your listener, convincing them of your Irish resonance.

Read the passage a final time, striving to pronounce the various changes, including the rise in pitch that occurs on both R-endings and the long U, as well as the shift from OU to AU, plus the short A lilting into the short O.

Mastery Lesson #3
(with annotations)

au ah

I'm here about Alison. I don't know where to begin.

ah

I've had a wee bit to drink.

    ↗   *ah*

I know that you and her have this long history. You

   ↗ ↗   *au*

were a large part of her life for a stretch, and now

   ↗   *ah*   *au*

you're here for her. I'm not daft. Right now she says

     ↗

she hates you, that you should die, and she never

wants to see you again. That's what she says right

au

now. But I know that one of these nights she'll be

                       ah

right where I am, looking you over with a nostalgic

64

ache in her heart. I thought I'd beat her to the punch

and come see you first.

I knew the whole story. I knew you left her. I always

figured you'd come back. But there are parts of this

that you aren't aware of.

ah   ah
Alison cracked up when you left. She refused to eat.

ah   ah
Had to be locked away for months. I met her last year

ah   ah   ah
when her mother passed, and Alison hadn't been with

au
anyone else. In six years, no one since you. Now, I

deal with grief every day. People walk into my shop

au   ah
in terrible states. But I see those people bounce back.

Even during the brief process of arranging a funeral,

ah

people begin to heal. Not so with Alison. The girl is

au

shaky. There are days when I leave the house, and I

ah

don't know if she's going to be there when I get back.

ah

I've buried many people. I don't want to add her to

my list.

I'm older than you. I've seen things I didn't care to.

They made me learn to look at a situation for what it

ah

is. As much as it hurts, I can admit that Alison isn't in

love with me.

ah   ah

If you win Alison back, so be it. I'll let her go. But if

you came here for kicks, to seduce her and then pull

ah   ah

your vanishing act, I'm warning you I won't take

kindly to it. Another disappointment would kill her.

ah   ↗   *ah*
If I have to bury her, I'll cremate your skinny ass and

        ah
dump your ashes.

68

Miscellaneous Tips

Change *It is* to *'Tis*
God gives you the cow, Terry, but *'tis* the Devil that gives you the knife.
'Tis some concept.
'Tis quite important to have enemies.
'Tis something that isn't found very often.
'Tis a crying shame.
'Tis a tedious task.
'Tis a decision I had to make.

Change *It was* to *'Twas*
'Twas a once in a lifetime occurrence.
'Twas Deborah who had Sean come to you.

Change *It isn't* to *'Tis not*
'Tis not my most productive evening.

Change *It wasn't* to *'Twas not*
Despite my efforts, *'twas not* my best-selling title.

Following a suspicious death, the Irish do not perform an *autopsy*. They refer to the procedure as a *post mortem*.

When speaking of a future date, the Irish wouldn't say *next Sunday*, they would say *Sunday week*.

If an Irishman tries to fool someone, they aren't *putting someone on*, they're *having them on*.

Are you serious about taking the mail to the post, or are you *having me on?*

An Irish engineer might carry a flashlight, but he refers to it as a *torch*.

When an American wishes to express his happiness for someone, he might say "<u>Good</u> for <u>you</u>." On the other side of the Atlantic, an Irish would say, "Good <u>on</u> you."

Acting with an Irish Brogue

This section is reserved for performers seeking to use the accent for an upcoming role. It is intended to shed light on the complicated and intriguing Irish mystique.

Ireland is an island in the North Atlantic to the west of Great Britian. Many things are associated with Ireland, including stout, a kind of porter beer, the most popular in America being Guinness. The American mind, when hearing the word 'Irish', also jumps to St. Patrick's Day, Lucky Charms cereal, the color green, leprechauns, and a pot of gold waiting at the end of the rainbow.

A performer approaching an Irish character has greater considerations, most notably the emotional sensitivity and availability of the Irish.

The culture has dealt with loss in many areas, facing political strife, religious conversion, invasions, conquests, a partition of the island, civil unrest, and the Great Famine of the 1840s. Because of their long history of travails, Irish people are often deeply in touch with their pain, and can access it to great affect, including to charm the object of their desire, arouse sympathy, or make a point. An actor that chooses to employ an Irish brogue should be aware of its power.

73

Sources for Future Reference

Film: *The Crying Game, This is My Father, The Playboys, In the Name of the Father, Calvary*

Audiobooks: *Angela's Ashes, 'Tis*

Sinead O'Connor and U2 - when they speak on their albums

75

Final Notes

When attempting to learn an accent, we're all humbled by how difficult and beguiling it can be.

I value your time enough to provide you with simple goals, which include focusing on one vowel change at a time, then tackling a handful of changes during the mastery lessons.

The bigger goal is to free your creativity. The vowel changes offer perspective, but it takes a bit of art to handle the accent with a sensibility that listeners trust.

Study the guidelines, then play with the dialect. When you make it your own, you'll be able to change the mood of a room with only a few carefully placed—and Irish-infused—words.

The author intends to make support for this publication available online. At the time of this writing, YouTube is the most popular site for posting videos that demonstrate chapters of this book.

To find online lessons, search **IvanBorodin** and/or **Learn an Irish Brogue** on YouTube.

The author recognizes the Internet as an evolving beast. Should another site become the leader in social media, please search for support for this book using the tags listed above.

About the Author

Ivan Borodin has taught accents since 1996 at Los Angeles' City and Valley Colleges. He works as a Hollywood dialect coach, and has appeared on televison performing various accents.

The obsession with speech started when he was a young New Yorker. Typecast as a product of his native Queens, he thought of nothing except how to create the illusion of being from someplace else. This intense relationship with the topic of speech expanded his range as an actor, and led him to teach the subject.

Accents are a novel and intriguing aspect of storytelling. Borodin hopes this manual empowers you to develop a stellar Irish brogue, and that it becomes another option in expressing your unique voice.

Borodin continues to teach privately, both in his home in Los Angeles and via telephone and Skype worldwide.

Ivan Borodin

1626 N. Wilcox Avenue #490

Los Angeles, California 90028

IvanPresents@gmail.com

office (323) 319-4826

Skype handle: IvanBorodinUSA

About the Illustrator

Pete Sain is a freelance designer. He has done artwork and layouts on numerous novels and instructional manuals. He specializes in the creation of novelty products, many of which can be found on zazzle.com under his brand name *godofapathy*. Mr. Sain writes fiction, is a lifelong student of art and science, and lives in Victoria, British Columbia.

Also by Ivan Borodin

Speak with an Accent
Explore the full range of a dozen accents (Australian, French, Russian, Southern, German, British, New York, Scottish, Cockney, Japanese, Arabic—as well as Irish!) on this Compact Disc. An absolute must-have for character actors.

Speak with a New York Accent
In the Big Apple, you keep your head down and avoid eye contact with strangers. But when you decide to talk like a New Yawka, you better bring the necessary vowel and consonant changes—and the attitude. Forgetaboutit!

Learn a Southern Drawl
Everyone has their version of a Southern accent, but with this manual, you'll have the one born of pure Dixie charm.

Learn a Wicked Awesome Boston Accent
No dialect carries the authenticity and moral righteousness of a straight-up Boston accent. As a bonus, this book will help you sound wicked awesome.

Speak with an African Accent
Maximize your practice time with this concise guide. Key vowel and consonant changes are outlined in a strategic manner, allowing the reader to gain speedy confidence. Designed by master dialect coach Ivan Borodin, this handbook serves as an introduction to the pronunciation shifts needed to speak with a convincing African accent.

Learn a Scottish Burr
Whether you're an actor preparing for a role, a fan of the cinema, or just obsessed with accents, this manual is for you. Master Dialectician Ivan Borodin takes you through a series of easy-to-follow drills that ease you into this unique and popular dialect.

Also by Ivan Borodin and Pete Sain

Accent Annihilation for Japanese Speakers
An illustrated handbook for those born in the land of the rising sun who wish to speak American English with a clear accent. Focusing on syllable stress and the production of key consonants and vowels, this is the perfect guide to not only reducing your accent, but annihilating it!

Made in the USA
Middletown, DE
06 June 2018